P9-DBM-270

AMERICAN INDIAN LIFE

The Powhatan

The Past and Present of Virginia's First Tribes

by Danielle Smith-Llera

Consultant:
Brett Barker, PhD
Associate Professor of History
University of Wisconsin–Marathon County

CAPSTONE PRESS
a capstone imprint

Fact Finders Books are published by Capstone Press,
1710 Roe Crest Drive, North Mankato, Minnesota 56003
www.mycapstone.com

Library of Congress Cataloging-in-Publication Data
Names: Smith-Llera, Danielle, 1971- author.
Title: The Powhatan : the past and present of Virginia's first tribes / by
  Danielle Smith-Llera.
Description: North Mankato, Minnesota : Capstone Press, 2016. | Series: Fact
  finders. American Indian life | Includes bibliographical references and index. |
  Description based on print version record and CIP data provided by publisher;
  resource not viewed.
Summary: Explains Powhatan history and highlights Powhatan life in modern
  society.
Identifiers: LCCN 2015046716 (print) | LCCN 2015043524 (ebook) | ISBN
  978-1-5157-0239-9 (library binding) | ISBN 978-1-5157-0243-6 (pbk.) |
  ISBN 978-1-5157-0247-4 (ebook pdf)
Subjects: LCSH: Powhatan Indians—History—Juvenile literature. | Powhatan
  Indians—Social life and customs—Juvenile literature.
Classification: LCC E99.P85 (print) | LCC E99.P85 S65 2016 (ebook) | DDC
  975.5004/97347—dc23
LC record available at http://lccn.loc.gov/2015046716

Editorial Credits
Alesha Halvorson, editor; Richard Korab, designer; Tracy Cummins and Pam
Mitsakos, media researchers; Tori Abraham, production specialist

Source Notes
Page 22, line 1: H. Brevy Cannon. "Chickahominy Chief Tells Visiting Youth of
Education's Importance in Democracy." *UVAToday*. 14 Sept. 2014. 25 Jan. 2016.
https://news.virginia.edu/content/chickahominy-chief-tells-visiting-youth-
education-s-importance-democracy.

Photo Credits
Alamy: Dennis Tarnay Jr., 7; Capstone Press: 22; Corbis: Morgan Hill/Demotix,
21, 28; Getty Images: Buyenlarge, 25, Douglas Graham/Roll Call, 23; iStockphoto:
Dwight Nadig, cover (background), traveler1116, cover (top), 1; Native Stock
Pictures: Angel Wynn, cover; Newscom: Douglas Graham/Wild Light Photos,
27, Douglas Graham/WLPInc., 26; North Wind Picture Archives: 5, 8, 10, 12,
14, 15, 16, 17, NativeStock, 6, 9 (bottom); Shutterstock: Alyson L. Wright, 29
(background), Jill Lang, 4, Joseph Sohm, 9 Top, 13, 19, Rehan Qureshi, 28
(bottom right)

Printed and bound in China.
009464F16

Table of Contents

Working Together

Silvery fish, called shad, flop and twist in nets. Members of Powhatan tribes collect their eggs in special tanks. Within days, baby fish emerge. They feed on tiny shrimp, growing bigger. But the tribe members do not eat them. They release the shad into the river. Millions more fish inhabit rivers today because of Powhatan tribes.

Rivers fed their **ancestors** and connected their tribes during difficult times of change. Powhatan today work to protect their **traditions**—and healthy rivers—for their children and future generations.

ancestor: family member who lived a long time ago
tradition: custom, idea, or belief passed down through time

Powhatan fishing customs

Shad fishing is an important industry for the Powhatan and at the center of their culture. Modern fish hatcheries keep shad populations up, which the Powhatan harvest each spring.

The James River has always been important to the Powhatan people.

Chapter 1

The Confederacy

replicas of reed-covered dwellings at a Powhatan village in Jamestown, Viriginia

confederacy: union of people or groups with a common goal
council: group of people elected to make decisions for a larger group

A bronze engraving of Chief Powhatan is on display at the Pamunkey Reservation.

Water flows down the Blue Ridge Mountains, across plains, and into the Atlantic Ocean. In the 1600s Chief Wahunsonacock easily traveled the waters by canoe, visiting the villages he ruled in what is now Virginia. The English later called him Powhatan.

Chief Powhatan united more than 30 tribes into a powerful **confederacy**. Werowocomoco was the capital, which is in present-day Gloucester County. The chief protected more than 150 villages in exchange for tributes of food and gifts.

Tribes of the Powhatan Confederacy shared much in common. They lived near rivers in the Chesapeake Bay area. They spoke similar Algonquian languages. Each village had a leader who was usually chosen by Powhatan.

But the tribes were also independent. A **council** of advisers and priests helped their leaders make decisions for the villages. The Nansemond, Chickahominy, Pamunkey, Mattaponi, and Rappahannock peoples were loyal to the Powhatan Confederacy—but also to their own tribe.

VILLAGE LIFE

Every man, woman, and child helped the village survive. With bows and arrows, men hunted deer and turkey. They protected their villages in war. They caught plentiful fish with nets and spears. Dried fish and meat helped keep the tribes fed all winter.

Women scraped deerskin until it was smooth. They stitched skirts and shirts for themselves and **breechcloths** for men. Wealthy tribe members wore turkey feathers and river pearls. Families grew squash, beans, corn, and sunflowers in gardens. Children helped chase hungry animals away from the crops. In the forest they helped women gather nuts and berries. At the shore they helped collect oysters and crabs.

An illustration from the 1500s features Powhatan fishermen using spears to catch fish.

breechcloth: short deerskin clothes worn around the middle of the body

POWERFUL POWHATAN WOMEN

Women held great power in Powhatan villages. They owned the homes their families shared. They decided what food tribe members ate. Women connected the tribe to the past. Powhatan tribe members tracked their family history through female ancestors.

Women helped decide who would lead the tribe. When the chief died, his or her brother or sister could become the new chief. The chief's sisters' children could also rule—but not his or her brothers' children.

Today women are gaining more power as leaders of Powhatan tribes. They serve on tribal councils. The Rappahannock tribe elected G. Anne Richardson as chief in 1998. She was the first female chief to lead a tribe in Virginia since the 1700s.

Rappahannock Chief G. Anne Richardson with other Powhatan tribe leaders

Women helped build houses for their families. The hut-like homes were covered with sheets of bark. Inside, children helped women stir clay pots bubbling with stew over fires. Smoke escaped through an opening at the top of the dwelling.

inside a Powhatan lodge

A woodcut based on a 1585 painting features a Powhatan ceremonial dance. Some dances were used to celebrate the harvest season.

SENSE OF COMMUNITY

Powhatan villages helped each other. Villagers traveled by canoe to visit other tribes to trade goods for needed supplies. Sometimes they used white and purple shell beads, called wampum, as money.

Village **elders** taught children the tribe's history through stories and songs. Girls learned how to feed and clothe the village from their grandmothers and aunts. Grandfathers and uncles taught boys how to hunt. If a young male wanted to be closer to nature, he was put to the test—he had to live alone in the forest for months.

Elders taught young people to thank nature for its gifts. The tribe celebrated summer's ripe corn and fall's harvest. They returned bones of animals they ate to the forest or river. Elders also taught young people to trust nature to keep them healthy. Medicine-makers dressed in snake and weasel skins danced and sang to help sick tribe members recover. They made medicine from wild plants. They burned **sacred** tobacco to scare away the spirits they believed caused illness.

elder: older person whose experience makes him or her a leader
sacred: holy

Chapter 2

Powhatan Struggles

John Smith and the English colonists would bring huge changes to the Powhatan way of life.

Anniversary of Jamestown
Queen Elizabeth II of England visited Virginia in May 2007 for the 400th anniversary of Jamestown's founding. Eight chiefs of Virginia tribes proudly shook her hand at the Capitol building in Richmond. It was the first time the anniversary celebration included Virginia's tribe members.

Life changed for the Powhatan in 1607. Three ships carrying 104 English people arrived on the shore of the present-day James River. They were searching for good land—and gold and silver. Instead the travelers found mosquito-filled swamps with water too salty to drink.

Chief Powhatan helped the strangers. His people traded food and furs for metal tools and glass beads. They led the English to fresh water and showed them how to plant crops. The English busied themselves building the **colony** they named Virginia. Captain John Smith and others eagerly explored the surrounding area and named their first village Jamestown.

Hundreds more English settlers flooded into the colony. But supplies ran low. In 1610 colonists attacked villages to steal food. Angry Powhatan warriors fought back.

colony: an area settled by people from another country and controlled by that country

The English and the tribes made an agreement to stop fighting in 1614. Powhatan's daughter, Pocahontas, married Englishman John Rolfe. But both Powhatan and Pocahontas died a few years later. The agreement did not last.

Jamestown was growing, and colonists took over more Powhatan land. Powhatan's brother, Chief Opechancanough, led warriors in fierce attacks in 1622. They killed almost one-third of the 1,200 colonists. Furious Englishmen killed and captured tribe members. They burned their villages.

Colonists carried diseases that killed more Powhatan than gunfire. In 1607 the Powhatan Confederacy had more than 14,000 members. By the 1640s there were only 5,000.

Pocahontas married John Rolfe in Jamestown in 1614.

Chief Opechancanough and his followers fought a losing battle against the colonists.

The Powhatan Confederacy started to crumble in 1646. The English captured and killed Opechancanough. The new chief, Necotowance, signed a **treaty** with the English. The Powhatan agreed to obey England. They gave up much land shared by the confederacy. They agreed to live on small pieces of land called **reservations**.

treaty: an official agreement between two or more groups or countries

reservation: area of land set aside by the government for American Indians; in Canada reservations are called reserves

Life was difficult for the Powhatan in the 1700s. But many Jamestown colonists became rich. They grew tobacco to ship to England. There it sold for high prices. Colonists eagerly planted more—even on Powhatan reservations.

Tobacco was an important money-making crop for English settlers.

Ships carried tobacco from Virginia to England.

Powhatan lost or were forced to sell most of their lands. They were left with too little land to farm or hunt. Women sold handmade baskets to buy food. Men worked as hunting guides for the English. Many Powhatan, including children, worked as servants in English homes and on farms.

Without land, most Powhatan people could not live together like their ancestors had in the past. It became difficult for the Powhatan to practice their traditions together. Many wore English clothing, lived in wooden houses, and hunted with guns. They learned English and attended Christian churches.

TAKING A STAND

In the early 1900s Powhatan families living apart begin to organize themselves into tribes. They demanded that Virginia accept that tribes had their own traditions and history. Unfair laws made Virginia a difficult place to live for the Powhatan and other tribes. From the late 1800s until the 1950s, Virginia and other southern states did not allow whites and non-whites to go to school together or to marry each other. American Indians in Virginia suffered this **segregation** along with African-Americans.

In the 1950s and 1960s, African-Americans demanded fair treatment. Native American tribes across the United States united to demand respect and their rights too. Powhatan tribes are now grateful to these ancestors. They helped win the freedoms they enjoy today.

segregation: the practice of keeping groups of people apart, especially based on race

descendant: person who comes from a particular group of ancestors

INDEPENDENT TRIBES

The U.S. federal government recognizes 566 American Indian tribes. Powhatan tribes want the U.S. Congress to add them to this list. One such Powhatan tribe, the Pamunkey, finally achieved federal recognition in July 2015. But the decision is on hold pending court action.

It has been difficult for Virginia tribes to convince the U.S. Congress to recognize them. One problem is that the treaties the tribes made with England when Virginia was a colony are not recognized by the United States today.

The tribes struggle with another problem. In the mid-1900s unfair laws in Virginia made tribes nearly invisible. Powhatan parents could not list their children as Native American on birth certificates, for example. Today they cannot easily prove to the U.S. Congress that they are true *descendants* of Powhatan tribes

Several Powhatan tribes in Virginia still seek national recognition from the U.S. federal government.

Chapter 3

Powhatan Tribes Today

The state of Virginia recognizes eight tribes that once belonged to the Powhatan Confederacy. The tribes range from 120 members to about 1,000 members. They are the Pamunkey, Mattaponi, Upper Mattaponi, Chickahominy, Eastern Chickahominy, Nansemond, Rappahannock, and Patawomeck. About 3,500 people are members of Virginia's Powhatan tribes today.

In the 1600s Powhatan tribe members spread across nearly 8,000 square miles (20,700 square kilometers) of present-day Virginia. Today only the Pamunkey and Mattaponi tribes live on the homelands of their ancestors. Their reservations are the oldest in the United States.

Other tribes purchased land together, near the homelands of their ancestors. Members of the Chickahominy, Eastern Chickahominy, Rappahannock, and Upper Mattaponi tribes live in communities that range from 32 acres (13 hectares) to 25,000 acres (10,120 hectares).

Other tribe members have settled in cities in Virginia. Members of the Nansemond tribe live in Suffolk and Chesapeake. Some tribe

Members of the Nansemond tribe wear traditional clothing at a powwow.

members live outside Virginia. In the late 1800s some Powhatan people moved north. Their descendants live in Pennsylvania and New Jersey.

Lost languages

The Algonquian languages spoken by the Powhatan people are almost entirely lost. To try to recapture their ancestors' languages, some tribe members today study similar languages still spoken in the northern United States and Canada.

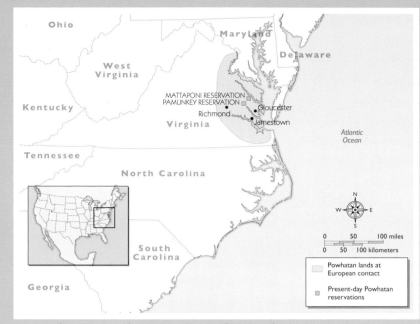

Powhatan reservations are located in Virginia.

GOVERNMENT

Many Powhatan tribe members live in "two worlds," according to Chickahominy Chief Stephen Adkins. They are **citizens** of the United States. But they are also citizens of their tribes.

Powhatan tribe members vote for Virginia governors, for example. But they also vote for their tribe's chief. They vote for members of the Virginia General Assembly, the group that makes laws for the state. But they also vote for members of the Tribal Council, which makes laws for the tribe.

Powhatan tribe members enjoy having a voice in their tribal governments. Chiefs still take advice from a council of leaders and elders.

RELIGION

Powhatan tribes lost most of their land more than 300 years ago. Yet their governments did not fall apart. Tribal councils met in churches. The Nansemond tribe has no tribal land, but their leaders still meet every month in a church.

Churches help the tribe members protect their history. They raise money and send volunteers to help the Pamunkey and Rappahannock tribes repair buildings built by their ancestors.

Church services connect Christianity with the beliefs of Powhatan ancestors. Church leaders compare the floods found in both the Bible and the stories told by their ancestors. Drumbeats might fill the church on Sundays. After holiday services tribe members might feast as their ancestors did—on shad from the river and cornbread.

Places for gathering

The Upper Mattaponi tribe gathers for meetings, events, and services at the Sharon Indian School and Indian View Baptist Church in Virginia's King William County—as their ancestors have done since 1919. They believe their tribe would not exist today without the two meeting places.

citizen: member of a country or state who has the right to live there

EDUCATION

Schools helped Powhatan people stay united during challenging times. The Powhatan struggled for many years to win their right to an education. Public schools emerged in the late 1800s, but the children of Virginia's tribes were not allowed to attend them with white children. Tribes built schools with the help of churches in the early 1900s. But the schools ended at the seventh grade. Parents had to send their children away to other states to continue their education.

In 1963 the future brightened for Powhatan people living in Virginia. The state finally allowed American Indian students to attend its public schools. The following year the first Powhatan doctor—from the Mattaponi tribe—graduated from medical school.

Today Powhatan people influence the education of all Virginia's students. Education officials work with chiefs and tribal councils to decide what schools teach. Public school students begin learning about Virginia Indian history and traditions in second grade.

From the late 1870s until the early 1920s, some American Indian students were allowed to attend Hampton Institute, an African-American school in Virginia.

Virginia colleges want American Indian children to study at their schools. Some college officials attract students with videos featuring American Indian college students, parents, and tribal leaders. Schools offer special programs for studying native history and scholarships to help pay for their studies.

Chapter 4

Connecting to the Past

Powhatan people today work as teachers, accountants, pharmacists, business owners, and many other occupations. Yet some choose the same jobs as their ancestors. Rivers still help some tribe members feed their families. Some people fish for food with fishing rods. Others, such as Patawomeck tribe members, weave baskets to catch eels like their ancestors did.

Powhatan fish for shad on the Mattaponi River.

Tribe members work hard to protect the rivers and fish their ancestors enjoyed. The Mattaponi and Pamunkey tribes have run shad hatcheries—places for hatching fish eggs—for almost 100 years. Tribe members also teach students and communities about keeping waterways clean and healthy for both fish and people.

Powhatan tribes also help train members for jobs outside their community. They learn to repair computers, do plumbing, work in hospitals, or teach at schools. But tribes encourage their members to stay connected to their people. Sometimes they pay for young tribe members' books and courses if they intend to choose jobs that help the tribe and its members.

PROTECTING RIVERS

Mattaponi people have always depended on the 85-mile (137-km) long Mattaponi River. Elders still teach young tribe members that the river gives life and has a spirit. They teach them to keep the river clean. They teach them how to fish but also how to help fish survive.

The health of the Mattaponi River was in danger in the early 1990s. The city of Newport News, Virginia, wanted to build a dam and reservoir to supply water to its residents. The project could disturb shad laying eggs. Flooding could swallow up parts of the reservation.

The Mattaponi, joined by the nearby Pamunkey and Upper Mattaponi tribes, began a 15-year battle to protect the river. They hired lawyers and argued against the project in court. The mayor of Newport News finally agreed to give up the project in 2009.

Mattaponi River in Virginia

CULTURE AND CRAFTS

Long ago Powhatan people gathered in their villages to celebrate harvests or battle victories. Today tribe members look forward to powwow celebrations. At the outdoor festivals, they celebrate traditions passed down by their ancestors.

Feathers and leather tassels twirl as dancers move to the rhythms of drums and turtle shell rattles. Storytellers repeat ancient tales. Artisans proudly display cane flutes, beaded jewelry, and belts.

Each year around Thanksgiving, crowds gather at the governor's mansion in Virginia. They watch as the Mattaponi and Pamunkey present wild game and gifts to the governor. The gifts honor their promise made in the 1600s to pay tribute to the Virginia colony. Powhatan today treasure their traditions—they are gifts from ancestors who worked hard to protect them for centuries.

Pamunkey pottery

Pamunkey artisans have run a pottery school on the reservation since the 1930s. Some potters make pots in traditional ways. They dig clay from the same riverbeds as their ancestors, and they avoid using modern tools.

TIMELINE

10,500 BC: Ancestors of Powhatan tribes arrive in what is now Virginia.

Late 1500s: Chief Powhatan forms and leads a confederacy of tribes.

1607: English colonists establish Jamestown inside Powhatan territory.

1610: Powhatan people and the English are at war until 1614; other wars rage from 1622 to 1626 and from 1644 to 1646.

1614: Powhatan's daughter Pocahontas marries the Englishman John Rolfe.

1616: Pocahontas, her husband, and son, and other Powhatan tribe members travel to England; she becomes ill and dies there in 1617.

1618: Chief Powhatan dies; his brother, Opechancanough, takes over as chief.

1646: Powhatan tribes begin to sign treaties with England that establish reservations.

1700s: The Rappahannock, Chickahominy, and Nansemond tribes lose their lands.

1800s: The Mattaponi and Pamunkey tribes hold on to their reservations; all other tribes living in Virginia lose their homelands.

1980s: Virginia recognizes seven tribes of the Powhatan Confederacy—Pamunkey, Mattaponi, Upper Mattaponi, Chickahominy, Eastern Chickahominy, Nansemond, and Rappahannock.

2009: President Barack Obama signs bill that includes text apologizing to American Indians for "many instances of violence, maltreatment, and neglect."

2010: Virginia recognizes the Patawomeck tribe.

2015: Pamunkey tribe receives federal recognition, but lawsuit puts decision on hold..

GLOSSARY

ancestor (AN-sess-tur)—family member who lived a long time ago

breechcloth (BREECH-kloth)—short deerskin clothes worn around the middle of the body

citizen (SI-tuh-zuhn)—member of a country or state who has the right to live there

colony (KAH-luh-nee)—an area settled by people from another country and controlled by that country

confederacy (kuhn-FE-druh-see)—union of people or groups with a common goal

council (KOUN-suhl)—group of people elected to make decisions for a larger group

descendant (di-SEN-duhnt)—person who comes from a particular group of ancestors

elder (EL-dur)—older person whose experience makes him or her a leader

reservation (rez-er-VAY-shuhn)—area of land set aside by the government for American Indians; in Canada reservations are called reserves

sacred (SAY-krid)—holy

segregation (seg-ruh-GAY-shuhn)—the practice of keeping groups of people apart, especially based on race

tradition (truh-DISH-uhn)—custom, idea, or belief passed down through time

treaty (TREE-tee)—an official agreement between two or more groups or countries

READ MORE

Benoit, Peter. *The Jamestown Colony.* Cornerstones of Freedom. New York: Children's Press, 2012.

Rajczak, Kristen. *The Life of Pocahontas.* Native American Biographies. New York: PowerKids Press, 2016.

Weil, Ann, and Charlotte Guillain. *American Indian Cultures.* Global Cultures. Chicago: Heinemann Library, 2013.

INTERNET SITES

FactHound offers a safe, fun way to find Internet sites related to this book. All of the sites on FactHound have been researched by our staff.

Here's all you do:

Visit *www.facthound.com*

Type in this code: 9781515702399

 Check out projects, games and lots more at **www.capstonekids.com**

CRITICAL THINKING USING THE COMMON CORE

1. Early Powhatan people depended on nature for food and faith. How is nature still a part of Powhatan tribe members today? (Key Ideas and Details)

2. Unfair laws made life difficult for Native Americans living in Virginia. In what ways are the lives of Powhatan tribe members better today? (Key Ideas and Details)

3. How do you think the United States would be different if Jamestown colonists had not met Powhatan tribes in the early 1600s? (Integration of Knowledge and Ideas)

INDEX